4/98

DRUGS AND EMOTIONS

Using drugs can make you feel like you are on an emotional roller coaster.

THE DRUG ABUSE PREVENTION LIBRARY

DRUGS AND EMOTIONS

Arthur Myers

THE ROSEN PUBLISHING GROUP, INC.
NEW YORK

Published in 1996 by The Rosen Publishing Group, Inc.
29 East 21st Street, New York, NY 10010

First Edition

Library of Congress Cataloging-in-Publication Data

Myers, Arthur.
    Drugs and emotions / Arthur Myers.
       p.   cm. — (The drug abuse prevention library)
    Includes bibliographical references and index.
    Summary: An overview of the psychological effects of such substances as nicotine, alcohol, cocaine, and amphetamines.
    ISBN 0-8239-2283-9
    1. Substance abuse—Juvenile literature.
2. Substance abuse—Psychological aspects—Juvenile literature. 3. Substance abuse—Prevention—Juvenile literature.   I. Title. II. Series.
HV4998.M94   1996
613.8—dc20

                        95-13902
                            CIP
                             AC

Manufactured in the United States of America

Contents

Introduction

Charles "Poncho" Brown works in the inner city of Boston, where he grew up. He lived the drug life, and now he talks to kids in schools about it. They listen to Poncho.

"It doesn't matter," he says, "if you're living in the inner city or in a million-dollar home in the suburbs. Drugs will [ruin your life] no matter where you are, or where you come from. Drugs are an equal opportunity to destroy you. Drugs don't discriminate.

"When I was in high school, I was using drugs recreationally. A little bit. I was a star athlete in basketball and football. I was scoring thirty points a game, or three touchdowns in football. I was

sniffing dope after the game, and gradually I ended up with a drug habit.

"Kids don't know what addiction is. They don't realize that you start off with half a joint or half a beer and you're high, but two weeks later you need more, and more, and more, and more. Kids need to know what road they're traveling.

"I had fourteen college scholarships offered to me. Instead, I went out selling drugs to support my own habit. I had a crew of ten or twelve people working for me. I'm not proud of what I did then. I'm proud of what I do now.

"I've talked to half a million people. I've been on *60 Minutes*. I teach doctors and Ph.D.s at Harvard, but most of all I like to speak to kids. I've got a degree in dopology. I've got a degree from the streets. Who else can better talk to kids about it than somebody who lived that life?

"I used to be proud of the problem. Now I'm proud of the solution."

Some teens use drugs to escape the problems they face in their lives.

CHAPTER 1

Getting into Trouble

Ronny is seventeen, but he looks older. He has a solid build and looks tough. But when he starts talking about drugs he reveals a very sensitive nature, a willingness to admit that he ran into a stone wall. He's desperately looking for a way around it.

Ronny has willingly spent months in a treatment center. It's a place where kids who have reached the end of the road, or gotten a good look at it, can live and learn and try to turn their lives around. A lot of them seem to be doing it. They seem as calm and hopeful as kids who have done heavy alcohol and drugs can be.

"I was twelve when I started using marijuana," Ronny says. "Everybody was using it. I started using it to get high, and because

10

so many other kids were doing it. But after a while I noticed that I needed to have pot every day. I was using it now to escape things that were bothering me: if I didn't have a good day in school or at home; if I'd done something wrong and knew I was in trouble. I would use marijuana just to escape reality. I wanted to be somewhere else, so I smoked some pot.

"Then I started escalating. I got into cocaine when I was fifteen, because after three years the pot wasn't working. I started snorting lines of cocaine. It was the thing to do in the crowd I was running with. I thought it was better than anything I'd ever done, alcohol or pot. With cocaine I had great highs.

"But then the depressions came. My life was like a roller coaster, emotionally up and down.

"When I was sixteen, I got into crack. It was my drug of choice for two years. It's taken me nowhere. It's taken me to the streets, to selling my body to men and women to make enough money to buy a fix. It's made me do things I normally wouldn't do— steal from my family, my friends, lie, manipulate. That's how far the disease of addiction will take you. I've slept outside and in abandoned houses. I've robbed people. All to get high. I've been in jails, in institutions.

Here, I'm starting to see what my life can *be without drugs."*

Teens and Drugs

One way of looking at drinking or taking drugs, says a psychologist who works with children and adolescents with heavy addiction problems, is that it's a kind of self-medication. It's not a tranquilizer that a doctor prescribes for you; it's something you give yourself.

"It's a method," he says, "to try to cope with sadness, frustration, pain, depression, rage. When kids first start to use drugs or alcohol, they experience peace, calm, happiness. Perhaps they had difficulty making friends, and all of a sudden there's a camaraderie around the drug culture. For many kids, it's the first time in their lives they've found a way to cope with unpleasant family situations, perhaps even physical abuse, sexual abuse, or emotional abuse. A whole variety of problems."

These kids experience a sense of well-being that they may not have felt before. Temporarily, they don't have to deal with real-life problems. But after a while they find that the drugs that allowed them to feel that happiness don't work as well.

12 | Like Ronny, they move on to drugs that give stronger highs. Many of these kids have poor self-esteem. Often they feel that they can't relate to others, that they are outsiders on the edge of society. They get excited by doing drugs. Sometimes this includes robbing people, stores, or homes, beating someone, or other violent criminal behavior. The reason for these crimes, in addition to needing the money to support a habit, is the excitement of committing a crime.

Drugs are powerful substances. They mask feelings that people don't want to experience. They free people from problems they don't want to deal with. However, none of these effects last very long. What does last are bad reactions. Depression, guilt, physical damage to one's body and emotions, and losing touch with reality are only some of the possible reactions people have to drug addiction.

Drugs disrupt the normal development of the body and mind. Teens who are addicted to drugs miss out on some very important years—the adolescent years. Adolescence is the time when people discover who they are, what they want to be like, what they want to do with their lives, and whom they want to spend time with.

Some teens start using drugs as a way to make friends.

Adolescence is also a time of great intellectual growth. None of this can happen if you're high on drugs or alcohol. If you're high, you can't concentrate, you can't focus, you can't learn.

The psychologist says, "Take a kid who is depressed, has no friends, is picked on at school and at home. Someone says, 'Have some of this stuff.' They smoke it and start giggling. The kid thinks, 'Gee, I've got a friend, it feels good, I'm going to do this a lot.' But an addict's friends are not real friends; they're just part of the addiction. They're there to borrow money, to trade drugs with, to buy drugs from or sell drugs to. Or maybe they just

14 | want to get someone else into the mess they are in. Misery loves company. Believe me, if you haven't got what they want from you, goodbye."

Alan is an only child. His father is a university professor; his mother is a social worker. He spent his early childhood in a commune, a place where many people lived together and drugs were a way of life.

"When we moved to a university town," Alan recalls, *"my parents hung around with various intellectuals. There were always people crashing at our house. I grew up around drugs. I grew up among adults. I never played with other kids. I learned to act very adult. If I had problems, I would pretend they didn't exist. I could explain everything away. But it didn't quite work.*

"I was teased a lot in school. The kids would call me 'nerd', or 'the human dictionary.' So, in an effort to become a cool guy, I started smoking marijuana, went for the punk-rocker clothes, and all that stuff. Once I started doing druggie stuff, the kids who were into that accepted me. I started selling drugs when I was in eighth grade. All of a sudden I was cool. I thought I had friends.

"I also found that if I was stoned all the

time I didn't have to deal with feelings. I always stayed away from alcohol because my mother is an alcoholic. I did a lot of halluci- nogenic drugs. I was a skinhead for a while. Then I started going to Grateful Dead con- certs. I was a Deadhead. I was selling a lot of drugs. I was tripping every day.

"I completely lost touch. A lot of the people I hung out with were going crazy. I decided to try to cool it. I decided I would become a beer connoisseur. I started drinking fancy types of beer. Pretty soon I had to drink so much to get drunk that I started taking pills with it. I was overdosing. I went into a coma for two days.

"I learned to suppress emotions early on. I had to act a certain way. I couldn't run around like a little kid, laughing, acting silly. So I learned how to keep emotions under control, to pretend they didn't exist. That's what drew me into drugs."

Adolescence and Change

As a teenager, your emotions are difficult to keep under control. Your body is changing. Your interests, talents, tastes, and friends may be changing as well. You probably question the rules and restric- tions your parents place on you. It is also likely that you question some of the

16 classes you take at school, the information you see on television, read about in books, newspapers, or magazines, and pretty much everything else in life. To sum it up, adolescence, the time of life you are now in, is when you begin to develop your own identity. You decide who you are, what you believe in, and what direction you want your life to take. This is a never-ending process which takes the rest of your life to complete, but it is during adolescence that the greatest strides are made.

Much of this change will affect and be affected by your emotions. Emotions are your feelings. Feelings can change from minute to minute. One minute you can be on top of the world and the next at the bottom, and never really know why. Perhaps it's because you did poorly on a test, or because you've moved to a new school and are finding it difficult to make friends. It could be that you are recovering from a bad breakup with a boyfriend or a girlfriend. Or you may feel that you just don't fit in, that your parents don't love you, or that no one understands you. It may be something even worse, such as physical, verbal, or sexual abuse at home. Whatever the reason, your emotions are

Some teens turn to drugs when they feel they have no control over their lives.

probably on something of a roller coaster ride.

People often turn to drugs or alcohol when they feel that they can't control their lives. They also look to these mind-altering substances to relieve pressure, forget about problems, fit into a crowd, or lose inhibitions. Whatever the reason, whatever feeling you are trying to control, be it depression, loneliness, anger, or anxiety, don't let drugs trick you into thinking they're going to help you. They won't. They can only hurt you. Drugs do not solve problems, they just create more problems.

CHAPTER 2

Dangers of Legal and Illegal Drugs

*M*ost people don't think of alcohol and nicotine as being drugs. But they are. And in most places in the United States, they are perfectly legal.

However, they are the most dangerous drugs in America, in terms of numbers of deaths they have caused. The U.S. Surgeon General has reported that smoking kills more than 320,000 Americans each year, from lung diseases, heart problems, and cancer.

Alcohol

After nicotine, alcohol is the second most deadly abused drug. It is reported that some 125,000 people die from drinking it in this country each year. Alcohol can damage the

Drinking alcohol can feel good at first, but it can also make you sick or cause you to pass out.

brain, the heart, the liver, and other vital organs. It is the cause of many fatal car accidents. Many of the drivers in those accidents are teenagers. It can cause birth defects and mental retardation in unborn babies of women who drink while pregnant.

Withdrawal from a serious drinking problem can be even more difficult and dangerous than getting off heavy drugs like heroin.

Yet you see people drinking and smoking all around you. We're surrounded by an ocean of TV shows, movies, and especially advertising that make smoking and drinking seem glamorous, cool, grownup, and fun.

19

Chewing tobacco, a popular habit among many professional
baseball players, can cause mouth cancer.

Drinking feels good at first. It relaxes you and gives you a high. It can also make you sick to the point of vomiting or it can make you black out. It becomes a habit that's very hard to break. It can make you do foolish things, such as getting behind the wheel of a car when you can't even walk. It can be deadly. It has been fatal for millions of people.

Drinking has increased among young people in recent years. Although the legal drinking age is twenty-one, many teens are able to get alcohol. Guidance counselors, teachers, and social workers estimate that some 70 percent of teenagers drink casually, usually on weekends. It's something kids see adults doing, and they want to copy it. For many kids, taking a drink is a sort of declaration of independence. But it's a step down a dangerous road.

Nicotine

On the positive side, fewer young Americans are now smoking than did ten years ago. The high level of publicity on the dangers of smoking has made both adults and teenagers think twice about taking nicotine into their mouths and lungs. And yet almost every day more than 3,000 young people begin smoking, starting a

22 │ journey that often leads to painful diseases and shortened lives.

Statistics indicate that every cigarette can shorten a person's life by 137 minutes. Nicotine clogs the arteries, affecting the entire circulatory system. This can lead to heart attacks and strokes. Smoking brings on respiratory diseases, such as emphysema, making it difficult for sufferers to catch their breath. Recent studies suggest that smoking increases women's risks of dying from breast cancer.

A person doesn't necessarily need to smoke tobacco to risk the dangers. Chewing tobacco, a tradition popular among many professional baseball players, can cause mouth cancer.

Billions of dollars are spent by tobacco producers to promote their deadly products despite the number of people dying from their use.

The public is becoming more and more aware of the dangers of nicotine. Fewer adults are smoking. Fifteen years ago, one could borrow a match from almost anyone in the office, at home, or on the street. Now few people have a light. Smoking is becoming rarer among adults.

To keep sales up, the cigarette industry has begun targeting young people, who

The tobacco industry uses ads like the Joe Camel campaign to target young people, who may be less informed about the dangers of smoking.

may be less well informed. The Joe Camel promotional campaign is a prime example of the tobacco industry's exploitation of young people. Studies show that just as many children recognize Joe Camel as who recognize Mickey Mouse. Cigarette ads show attractive, athletic young people having a wonderful time. The message is that they became good-looking, strong, and happy by smoking. The tobacco industry also concentrates on developing countries, where education is less extensive and young people are more easily lured into smoking.

Alcohol and nicotine are sometimes

24 | called gateway drugs. Through them, some young people move on to try marijuana and then harder drugs. It's a dangerous, downhill slide.

Marijuana

Compared with some drugs, marijuana may seem mild, but it can be dangerous. It is something to be wary of. Its many rather affectionate nicknames—"pot," "Mary Jane," "grass," "weed"—indicate how little it is feared by many people. But it frequently draws a young person into the heavier, more dangerous drugs.

Marijuana is made from the hemp plant, *cannibis sativa*. It's a mood-altering drug. Sometimes it pulls the user into a dreamy state of being "stoned." The mind becomes confused, time becomes distorted. A minute can seem like an hour, an hour like a minute. Gradually the "high" wears off, and moodiness and drowsiness set in.

Pot can be especially dangerous when taken with alcohol. The effect is tripled. Pot, beer, and driving have added up to many a fatal road accident.

Among regular users, sore throats and eventual lung damage are common. Health problems can add up in hidden ways. Pregnant women who use mari-

The basketball player Len Bias died the first time he tried cocaine.

juana risk having a premature or low birth-weight baby.

Constant users of marijuana frequently show a loss of motivation. They tend to "drop out"—to lose interest in their usual activities, both work and recreation. They change friends, drifting toward people who also use drugs.

Marijuana users frequently experience mood swings and irritability. Their attention spans shorten. Users seem constantly distracted. Their work and social lives are disrupted.

Marijuana is an escape from reality. Like other drug-based escapes, a person can be drawn in by subtle emotional

26 | difficulties and then introduced to some not-so-subtle ones.

Cocaine

For example, if you move on to cocaine or its even more deadly form, crack, you are flirting with real trouble. You can die quickly or slowly from this sort of poison. Len Bias is an example of how quickly cocaine can kill.

Bias was an outstanding basketball player at the University of Maryland. He had just signed on with the Boston Celtics, one of the leading teams in the National Baskeball Association (NBA). At twenty, he was about to become a millionaire. Celebrating his success with friends, he tried cocaine for the first time. A few seconds later, he was dead.

Cocaine is a white powder, usually smuggled from Central and South America. It is estimated that in the United States between 5 and 15 million people use cocaine regularly, and another 5,000 try it for the first time every day.

Some young people use crack. It's found in many schools. "A head of crack," says a school social worker, "is only about $5, less than the price of a movie, so it's easy to start." Once started,

it's easy to get hooked. Then it can become very expensive. A heavy crack habit
can cost $500 a day.

Cocaine is usually "snorted." This can
be very damaging to the inner tissues of
the nose. Continued use can create a hole
in the septum, the membrane between
the nostrils. The "high" or "rush" is
short-lived. The "crash" comes quickly.
Chronic users become depressed. They
find it hard to sleep. Cocaine is very addictive. It's difficult to stop using it.
Many cocaine users borrow money or,
when that runs out, turn to robbery and
burglary to support their drug habit.
Shoplifting often becomes a way of life
for cocaine users. So does time in prison.

Cocaine affects the brain. Panic attacks
and hallucinations are not unusual among
cocaine users. Users can become para-
noid, believing someone is out to harm
them or even kill them. They hear foot-
steps that don't exist. They see snakes
slithering in their beds. Cocaine can also
cause seizures that result in convulsions
and strokes. Cocaine can even cause users to suffer from heart attacks.

Crack
Crack is a more potent form of cocaine.

28 | It is made into white crystals that can be smoked. It is sold in small chips, sometimes called "rocks." It can be sprinkled into a cigarette or a marijuana joint. Crack is a concentrated form of cocaine that is extremely dangerous and addictive. A crack high lasts five to ten minutes. The crash is very rough, leaving the user tired, depressed, and irritable.

You go way up for a very short time, and then come *way down*. After the high, you feel so terrible that you have an overwhelming craving for more crack so you can get back up again. Crack is very hard to stop using. Addicts find the drug much more important than food. One teenage addict lost forty pounds in six months.

"You just feel ugly," he said. "You can't look in a mirror, because you know you look disgusting."

Heroin

Heroin is even worse than cocaine.

This powerful, addictive drug is produced from opium. Opium comes from the poppy plant, which is grown in warm parts of the world. Heroin is expensive. Some users sniff this whitish powder or inject it under the skin with a hypodermic needle. The most desperate addicts inject heroin directly into a vein. This is called mainlining. It can cause infections and damage the veins. A particularly dangerous aspect of mainlining is that users often share unsterilized needles. Through this practice, users risk the chance of becoming infected by HIV, the virus that causes AIDS.

Some people inhale the fumes of heated heroin. This is sometimes called "chasing the dragon." If you *catch* the dragon, it can be a grim experience.

Heroin sometimes makes a new user feel sick, but it can also produce a powerful high followed by a sense of relief from stress and worry. There is a saying about heroin: "It's so good, don't even try it once." It takes larger and larger doses to get high. Eventually there is no high at all, just a momentary relief from an almost overpowering craving.

Withdrawing from heroin is extremely painful, both mentally and physically. A person who is withdrawing experiences anxiety, sleeplessness, fear, and a desperate desire for the drug.

According to one inner-city teenager, "People think you're a basehead if you use heroin. Especially if you shoot up. But many kids in this school have people in their neighborhoods or families who

30 have that addiction. It's scary. The question kids keep asking themselves is 'How can I stay away from this, what can I do so that I don't get hooked?' "

Amphetamines and Barbiturates

Some drugs are legitimately prescribed by doctors to treat illnesses, but are also sold illegally on the street by drug dealers. These are amphetamines, often called "uppers," and barbiturates, called "downers." The uppers are stimulants; the downers are depressants. Both can be dangerous when not used under a physician's care.

These drugs are sometimes called "greenies" because of the color of the capsules they often come in. The drugs can also be obtained as powder, which is snorted. Sometimes it is injected with a needle, which involves the risk of contracting AIDS.

Uppers provide a powerful high—an excitement and energy. They also cause confusion and the inability to sleep. Uppers can cause brain damage or heart attacks. Many people have died from overdoses. Mixing uppers with alcohol has been fatal many times. Marilyn Monroe is believed to have died as a result of mixing alcohol with pills.

Barbiturates, or "downers," can make you feel very relaxed,
but they can also cause nausea, double vision, and slow reflexes.

32   Downers are particularly addictive. It is said to be more difficult to withdraw from them than from heroin. Sudden withdrawal can cause severe convulsions, sometimes even death. The drugs produce a dreamy, relaxed state. They also cause nausea, slurred speech, slow reflexes, double vision, and a lack of coordination and balance. The difference in the amount of the drug that produces sleep and the amount that kills is very small. As a result, countless people have died from overdoses of barbiturates.

Inhalants

A type of substance that is sometimes abused by children is inhalants. It is said that one in three children has used inhalants.

Inhalants include certain kinds of glues and other household products whose fumes cause a sort of intoxication, like drunkenness. Continual sniffing can result in brain damage, dizziness, confusion, and aggressiveness.

The chemical fumes from aerosol cans, model glue, cleaning fluids, paint sprays, gasoline and kerosene vapors can be mind-altering and sometimes fatal. Kids trying to get high on such substances

have been involved in violence and accidents. Some suffer serious burns when
the substances burst into flames. Children
have suffocated when using plastic bags
to concentrate the fumes. Others have
passed out and choked to death on their
own vomit.

Hallucinogens

Another class of illegal substances is
hallucinogens. These drugs are sometimes
called psychedelic, which means mind-
expanding. Perhaps the most widely
known of such drugs is LSD, short for
lysergic acid diethylamide. It is also called
"acid." This drug was very popular in the
1960s, in the days of Flower Children
and communes. It is a fad with some
teenagers today to romanticize the '60s.
"Dropping acid"—swallowing LSD on a
sugar cube or small tablet—is sometimes
part of this fad.

Taking LSD is also called "tripping." The
trips can be very unpredictable. They can
be very frightening. People panic, become
violent, or get involved in accidents.

One of the really scary aspects of an
LSD trip is that it can recur over and over
again without further doses of the drug.

Another hallucinogen common in

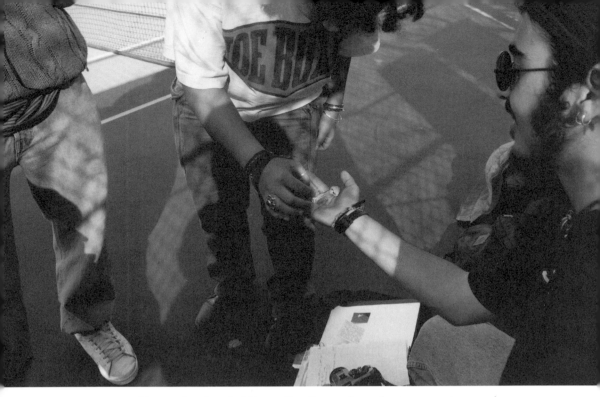

If you develop habits easily, it may be safer to never try smoking, drinking, or other drugs.

schools today is psychedelic mushrooms, often called "shrooms." These mushrooms contain a drug similar to LSD. They used to be called "magic mushrooms." The magic, however, is not guaranteed to be beautiful. Sometimes it can be horrible.

A drug sometimes confused with hallucinogens is PCP (phencyclidine). It is made in illegal laboratories, usually in somebody's garage or cellar. PCP comes either as a pill or as a powder. The powder form, which is sometimes called "angel dust," is snorted. It makes the user feel passive and disconnected. Other effects are rubbery legs, dizziness, nausea, and, sometimes, uncontrollable terror.

CHAPTER 3

When You're in over Your Head

Liza is an attractive, charming young woman of seventeen. She is a high school graduate, friendly in manner, articulate in speech. One would never guess when meeting her that her entire life is devoted to staying away from alcohol and drugs and trying to help other people do the same.

Liza goes to Alcoholics Anonymous meetings every evening. During the day, she works as a volunteer for a hot line, a phone number people call when they need help to break free from their problems. They call in for help, and she talks to them. They listen to her, because she gives them hope.

Liza started drinking when she was thirteen years old. She lived in a small town in Pennsylvania and was close friends with two

36 *other girls. One day they decided to try drinking beer.*

"The three of us split a case," she recalls.

Liza is still in touch with her two friends. They never became addicted to alcohol or drugs. They are looking forward to having careers, marriages, and children. They lead what society considers normal lives. They can take a drink or leave it.

But Liza was hooked on alcohol and other drugs all through her early youth. These days, Liza's life is centered around staying off the various poisons she used.

Liza has an addictive personality. "It runs in my family," she says. "I think that even at thirteen I was an alcoholic just waiting to pick up a drink. I think I was born this way."

Liza belongs to that unfortunate group of people who easily become addicted to bad habits. There is a phenomenon that workers in the helping professions call cross-addiction. If you are easily pulled into such ways of coping with life or handling difficult emotions, you may use pot in your teenage years and cocaine and heroin later on. Or you may turn to overeating, or dieting yourself into a skeleton. People like this can become addicted to abusive relationships, to going overboard on shopping, even to overdoing exercise. These are all addictions that an addictive personality is prone to.

Addiction can develop gradually in a person. A man may have no obvious trouble with drinking or smoking pot for years. He gets an education, holds a job, gets married, and has a family. One day his wife asks him to stop drinking his evening cocktails, because he's disrupting the family. He realizes that those evening drinks—unwinding time, as he calls it, his way of coping with the tensions of the day—are something he can't do without. His wife may eventually take the children and leave, or ask him to leave the house. He wonders what happened. He has become addicted, and his life has fallen apart.

Being prone to addiction can be something physical. It may be a gene passed down from a parent. Or it can be environmental—the neighborhood and society one lives in, or one's particular family environment.

One expert put it this way: "With some people it's as if a pilot light was lit when they were born. All you have to do is turn up the gas. If they get into the

38 | wrong situation, it's as if the gas was turned up. Then they become dependent on the drug."

Another therapist says: "You know what makes people like that use drugs? They're happy, or they're sad, or they flunked a test, or they got an A. Or it's raining, or the sun is shining, or they're celebrating, or someone died. They go to someone's wake who overdosed on heroin, and they cry for five minutes. Then they go out and get high. They're feeling so low that they're going to get high. The feeling is built-in."

But plenty of kids get hooked even though they have no such built-in physical, possibly genetic trait. Sometimes it's just living in a certain place, being surrounded by a certain way of life. The environment gets them off on a dangerous track.

"There are many more people in the inner cities," a social worker says, "so the problem is magnified. It becomes part of the culture. You have ten- or twelve-year-old kids selling crack on the streets. It's not unusual, it's part of their cultural norm; they've grown up with it all their lives. In the inner city, some people get drunk every day and there's violence and

Drugs and violence exist everywhere. They are more visible in the inner cities, but they also exist in the suburbs.

fighting. It's all open to a kid growing up there.

"In the suburbs, it is more hidden, but the same situations can be involved. You'll have a family man living in a big house, a successful professional. But he's abusive to his wife and children. Everything looks great from the outside; but inside, forget it. One daughter has been physically and sexually abused. The son drinks. Another daughter flees to the West Coast to escape the family. The wife becomes addicted to prescription medicine."

Addiction is not limited to any one part of society. As Poncho Brown says, it doesn't discriminate.

40   Why did Liza get hooked on alcohol
and drugs when her two friends did not?
Was it physical, was it something in her
emotional set-up, was it problems in relationships with people? These situations
have no easy answers; it could have been
a combination of things.

Adolescence is a time of instability
under almost any circumstances. Who am
I today, who will I be tomorrow? It is a
time of new, sometimes confusing and
anxiety-filled experiences. It is a time of
searching, a time of curiosity. It's a time
of experimentation. That's normal. Of
course, it depends on what you're experimenting with.

Liza says, "I was curious. Booze and
drugs were around me, even in our small
town. I wanted to experiment. I was very
angry at that time. My stepfather was
physically, emotionally, and mentally abusive to my brother and me. Drinking, I
very quickly discovered, was an escape.
Of course, it was not really an escape. It
was a trap."

Some addictive-type people realize
quickly that they can't afford to take
drugs in any way, because they know they
can become hooked. One woman in her
seventies says, "I knew the very first drink

I took, when I was young, that I was out of control." She stayed away from drinking all her life.

Another woman, now in her sixties, saw her father, her sister, and her two sons become hooked on alcohol and drugs. She got the message early, as a teen. All her life, she has abstained from these poisons. It was obvious to her that she could easily become hooked herself.

But many people drink for years socially, recreationally, and then they step over an invisible line. They're caught; they've lost control. They've lost the power to decide. With Liza, drinking quickly became a way of life.

"All the friends I had drank like I did," she recalls, "partied like I did through high school. Those were the people I chose to hang out with—the druggies and the party animals. That becomes your identity.

"I got into LSD, speed, and cocaine. You can develop an addiction to crack in a week. With alcohol, you can drink for years, and then you cross a line and it just takes over your life. You have built up so much denial about it. You've been telling yourself all along, I'm okay, I'm okay, I'm okay!"

It's natural to be curious and want to experiment with different things in your teens, but experimenting with drugs or alcohol can lead you down a path of destruction.

Carlos lived in a suburb of a large city. Most of the boys in the neighborhood were older than him. He had a hard time being part of the gang. "They had clubhouses out in the woods," he recalls, "and sometimes they'd let me go out with them. They were drinking wine. I wanted to be one of the bunch, so I started drinking. I was about nine then. They got a big kick out of seeing this little kid knocking back wine. They gave me praise, approval. Then I started smoking cigarettes. I began to think the older kids liked me, that smoking and drinking kind of made me popular, put me in the club.

"When I was twelve, I started smoking pot, and pretty soon I started doing other things. I began to get into trouble. I got arrested for drinking in public. I'd come home and start breaking things up. I'd be whacked out. I'd start hitting on my family, my brothers and sisters and my mother.

"I was in and out of halfway houses and hospitals. I got suspended from school maybe twelve times. Finally, when I was seventeen, I was sent to a state prison for thirty days. That was really heavy. You're surrounded by people who are filled with hate. I was threatened with rape. It was a very scary place to be.

"I realized that for years I'd been on a

The happiness you feel when you're high is fake; your problems will be waiting for you when you come down.

constant run because I couldn't deal with my feelings. I was on a downhill slide. I couldn't let people get close to me. My father used to tell me, 'You've got to be tough all the time; you can't show your feelings.' I tried to be that way. I didn't want people touching me; I couldn't deal with people. But drugs sure weren't the answer. I know that now. But how could I let go of them, where could I turn? I was desperate."

44

CHAPTER 4

Getting Out of It

*I*t isn't easy.

Poncho Brown, who lived the drug life and who now devotes himself to keeping kids out of it, knows about getting off drugs. He says:

"You still like the high; that's what kills most addicts. You know you shouldn't be doing this, you're never going to have any kind of life, you're smarter than this. But you feel so lousy when you're coming off. The drugs are leaving your body and you come crashing down. You've got to get back up.

"There's the withdrawal beast. You're sick, you feel lousy, you'll do anything to get your drug—rob, kill, sell your body— anything to get money for drugs."

46

Liza knows the withdrawal route well. "Drinking, drugs, they were fun for a while," she says. "Then slowly but surely they started to ruin things. There was a lot of anger and a lot of fear. I didn't think I'd be able to quit. That was really terrifying. I got two DUIs (violations for driving under the influence of alcohol). I was sent to rehab centers. I was very defiant, very much the rebel. If anybody tried to tell me what I was doing, I'd just cut them off. It was all because of fear. I was afraid of what was going to happen to me. Terror is the big emotion when you have to quit. You're so afraid you won't be able to quit."

Recovery

One psychologist who works with addicts says: "Once an addict, always an addict. One can never recover, one can only be *in recovery*. It's a lifetime battle. For an addict, the craving is always there.

"When you're using drugs, you have no feelings that make any sense. Some people feel rage, lose control, and do violent things. The drugs mask most feelings. But the happiness that is induced by the drugs is an artificial happiness. The high masks feelings of hurt and sadness and

People who are hooked on drugs often do things—such as stealing—that they normally would not do if they were not addicted.

48 depression. The person really is not in touch with what is going on.

"They act out—get involved in crimes and violence against people. Or they act in—get very depressed, suicidal, in and out of psychiatric hospitals. But they can't give up their drug use. For an addict, life is a roller coaster—way up, then crashing way down."

People who are not addicts have frightening experiences with drugs and alcohol as well. Anyone who drinks too much alcohol or takes too much of a drug, or even mixes drugs and alcohol, can die from it. People who are high and physically acting out sometimes wind up in jail. Sometimes these people are thrown out of their homes; sometimes their boyfriends or girlfriends leave them. There are many consequences to drinking and abusing drugs.

Once someone is addicted to drugs or alcohol, it is a real struggle to quit. Quitting, or recovery, involves mental, physical, and emotional pain. The body tries to stabilize itself, to cleanse itself, and work normally again. This causes periods of depression, rage, and anger. These emotions can be aimed at oneself or at others. Some addicts may feel depressed about

the life drugs have led them to. Most
addicts will tell you that they are angry as
well, and it's usually anger at themselves
for being an addict.

A school social worker says, "When
their minds start to clear, addicts start to
think about the things they've done to
other people, what they've done to their
families. I see kids who have killed people. While they were doing it, under the
influence of drugs, they didn't see it as a
problem. It was as routine as putting on a
pair of glasses. Now their conscience be-
gins to come back. Or they may be finding a conscience for the first time in their
lives. And that can be very painful, to
have to deal with the things they have
done to others, or begin to remember the
things done to them.

"Some of these kids have been sexually
or physically abused. Some were turned
on to alcohol and drugs by family mem-
bers. Some, at the ages of four and five,
have sat in a room while their parents and
friends smoked marijuana. You can get a
contact high just sitting in a room full of
smoke.

"The pain of recollection is just unbe-
lievable. And there's the day-to-day struggle against the craving, because the body

50 and mind are still craving the drugs. I've listened to hundreds of kids and adults talk about this."

What is it like to stop using drugs or alcohol?

Ronny says: "You've got to surrender. Just say, I give up. You have to admit to yourself that you've got a big, big problem. You've got to realize: I can't do anything, I can't go to school, can't get a job, can't have healthy relationships. Not unless I'm clean.

"My life sucked when I was using, especially the last year. It was terrible. But sometimes the thought that I'll never use drugs or drink again for the rest of my life, it's too much to think about. So I do what they urge in Alcoholics Anonymous—take it one day at a time. That way I can stand it, and maybe make it work.

"What could the future hold? Well, I'd like to help other people with problems, with this addiction, if I can get hold of this recovery."

Alan says, "I think of going to college, maybe even becoming a professor like my father and my uncles. But I don't have much confidence in myself. Whenever I start becoming successful at something, that's when I try to find a way to mess myself up. I think it's because of having a poor self-image, low self-esteem. I feel I'm not good enough to deserve success, so I start doing these horrible things to myself. I've still got my hopes, though. You've got to have hope."

Carlos says, "With this addiction thing, you're never sure you've licked it. You can get over the physical part of it, the body's need for it—maybe. But you're never sure you're over the psychological craving. The best thing to do is stick with the teachings of Alcoholics Anonymous (AA), or Narcotics Anonymous (NA). Take it one day at a time.

"It's the emotional part that's so hard. I'm off drugs now, my physical addiction is gone, but there are times when out of nowhere I think about getting high. When that happens, I think of what the consequences would be. It'll take a while, a long while, to get clear of the emotional side of it. It never really goes away."

Liza says, "I haven't had a drink for months now. For many years I drank every day. AA has helped me a lot. AA gives your life structure. I listen to the other people, and it's like a big support

Alcoholics Anonymous and other support groups provide help and encouragement to recovering addicts.

group. You gain long-term friends, and they help you stay sober and off drugs, they help you stay clean. It's the fellowship. It's almost like a church, in a way.

"It's different from the people you hung out with when you were drugging. Those are not real friends. They're just people you buy drugs from, or sell drugs to, or trade drugs with. If you haven't got something to offer them, they disappear.

"Kicking the habit is different for everybody. For some, it's still tough and may never ease up. But a lot of people go on a thing called the pink cloud. Things are working for them. Compared with when they were into drinking and drugs, things are wonderful. They're being re-born. They're getting their fears and re-sentments out of themselves."

One psychologist says, "The percent-age of people who stay in recovery over a lifetime is much smaller than those who don't. But you can go anywhere in the world and find an AA meeting. There are at least fifteen AA meetings going on in this city at this moment. There are thou-sands and thousands of people out there who attend, whether it's AA or NA. In NA, the procedure and techniques are the same as in AA, but they talk more about narcotics. There are millions of people all over the world who attend these meet-ings, but there are even more millions who should.

"Some people go to AA or NA four or five times a day. When they first start out, sometimes that's the only thing they can do. They have to keep going to meetings and being with people who are in recov-ery. Over a period of time they begin to become stronger.

"Treatment centers use other activities to help people along in recovery. We take our kids to an NA campout. There are meetings for three days and all kinds of

54 enjoyable activities, so kids and adults can have fun in recovery. You can still ski if you're in recovery. You can go to the movies; you can go to a baseball game; you can play football. You have to learn to replace the pleasure you had while using drugs with the fun of normal life."

Glossary
Explaining New Words

AIDS (acquired immunodeficiency syndrome)   An incurable disease caused by HIV (human immunodeficiency virus), a virus usually acquired through sexual contact or by exposure to contaminated blood through hypodermic needles.

articulate   The ability to express oneself in clear, effective speech.

camaraderie   A spirit of friendliness and togetherness.

coma   State of deep, often prolonged unconsciousness, usually the result of injury, disease, or poison.

connoisseur   Person with expert knowledge or taste.

cultural norm   Behavior that is considered typical, or normal, in the society in which a person lives.

emphysema   Severe disease of the lungs, often caused by smoking.

escalate   To increase or intensify, as in the use of stronger drugs.

56 | **exploitation** Use of a person or group
for selfish, often harmful purposes,
often through advertising and publicity
campaigns.

genetic Handed down from one's an-
cestors through the genes one inherits.

hallucination False perception of ob-
jects or events, often as a result of
drug use.

joint Slang for a marijuana cigarette.

stoned Slang for being intoxicated,
under the influence of alcohol or a
drug.

Help List

Some people who have a problem, such as drug or alcohol addiction, would prefer to talk about it face-to-face with an informed adviser. Other people would rather seek help in a less self-revealing way—over the telephone, for example, or by writing a letter.

For the former, there are one's parents, although they may be literally too close to home. A favorite teacher might be able to advise you, or at least point you in the direction of someone who can. A school counselor, a clergyperson, a psychotherapist, or therapists who specialize in problems of addiction might be helpful. Some of your friends and schoolmates might have useful ideas or their own experiences in seeking help.

But if you would rather keep your distance, there is always the telephone. You'll find the people working for hot lines or help organizations to be sympathetic and knowledgeable. And they will not try to find out who you are, unless you want them to know.

The 800 numbers can be called without charge. A number with an area code means there will be a fee. If you don't want the call to appear on your home telephone bill,

58 gather up some quarters and call from a public telephone booth.

If you want to call a place in your own area, look in the Yellow Pages of the telephone book under such headings as Alcoholism, Drug Abuse, Counselors, and Religious Organizations.

Here are some suggestions:

Hot Lines

International Institute on Inhalant Abuse
   (303) 788-1951
"Just Say No" Kids Club (800) 258-2766
Marijuana Anon (800) 766-6779
Nar-Anon (310) 547-5800
National Institute on Drug Abuse (800)
   662-HELP
Youth Crisis Hot Line (800) 448-4663

Organizations

Al-Anon Family Group Headquarters, Inc.
1600 Corporate Landing Parkway
Virginia Beach, VA 23454-5617
(804) 563-1600

Alcoholics Anonymous
Box 459
Grand Central Station
New York, NY 10163
(212) 870-3400
e-mail: 76245-2153@compuserve.com

National Black Alcoholism Council, Inc.   *59*
285 Gennesee Street
Utica, NY 13501
(314) 798-8066

**National Clearinghouse for Alcohol and
    Drug Information**
P.O. Box 2345
Rockville, MD 20847-2345
(301) 468-2600
web site: http://www.health.org
e-mail: info@prevline.health.org

**National Council on Alcohol and Drug
    Dependence (NCADD)**
12 West 21st Street
New York, NY 10010
(212) 206-6770
(800) 622-2255

National Abuse Center
5530 Wisconsin Avenue, NW
Washington, DC 20015
(800) 333-2294

**Resource Center on Substance Abuse
    Prevention and Disabilities**
1819 L Street, Suite 300
Washington, DC 20036
(202) 628-8080
(800) 628-8442

| # IN CANADA

Addictions Foundation of Manitoba
1031 Portage Avenue
Winnipeg, MB R3G OR8
(204) 944-6200

Al-Anon Family Group
National Public Information
P.O. Box 6433
Station J
Ottawa, ON, K2A 3Y6
(613) 722-1830

Alberta Alcohol and Drug Abuse Commission
2nd Floor, 10909 Jasper Avenue NW
Edmonton, AB T5J 3M9
(403) 427-4275
e-mail: AADAC@freenet.edmonton.ab.ca

Narcotics Anonymous
P.O. Box 7500
Station A
Toronto, ON M5W 1P9
(416) 691-9519

Youth Detox Program
Family Services of Greater Vancouver
504 Cassiar Street
Vancouver, BC V5K 4M9
(604) 299-1131

For Further Reading

Berger, Gilda. *Addiction*. New York: Fanklin Watts, 1992.

———. *Making Up Your Mind About Drugs*. New York: E. P. Dutton, 1988.

Buckalew, M. W., Jr. *Drugs and Stress*. New York: Rosen Publishing Group, 1993.

Campbell, Chris. *No Guarantees*. New York: Macmillan, 1993.

Chomet, Julian. *Cocaine and Crack*. New York: Franklin Watts, 1987.

Condon, Judith. *The Pressure to Take Drugs*. New York: Franklin Watts, 1990.

Johnson, Gwen, and Rawls, Bea O'Donnell. *Drugs and Where to Turn*. New York: Rosen Publishing Group, 1993.

Mooney, Al J., and Eisenberg, Arlene and Howard. *The Recovery Book*. New York: Workman Publishing, 1992.

Myers, Arthur and Irma. *Why You Feel Down and What You Can Do About It*. New York: Charles Scribner's Sons, and Atheneum, 1982.

62 | Myers, Arthur. *Drugs and Peer Pressure.*
New York: Rosen Publishing Group,
1995.

Rosenberg, Maxine B. *On the Mend.* New
York: Bradbury Press, 1991.

Ward, Brian. *Drugs and Drug Abuse.* New
York: Franklin Watts, 1987.

Index

64

About the Author

Arthur Myers is an experienced investigative reporter who has won several prizes for newspaper writing and who at one time was an editor on the Washington Post. He has published some twenty books, about half of them for young people.

Mr. Myers lives in Wellesley, Massachusetts.

Photo Credits

pp. 8, 13, 34, 42 by Yung-Hee Chia; p. 25 © A/P Wide World Photos; p. 52 by Katherine Hsu; all other photos and cover by John Novajosky